Golden Linings

Tiny Tales about Pets, for Pets

Copyright © 2018 Carol M. Ford

ISBN: 978-1-943201-16-7

Library of Congress Control Number: 2018946383

Graphic Design by Darin M. Peters.

All rights reserved. No part of this publication may be reproduced or transmitted in any form or by any means, electronic or mechanical, including photocopying, recording, or any information storage and retrieval system without the written permission of the author.

First published by AM Ink Publishing: July 15, 2018.

AM Ink Publishing
15 Southwick Hill
Southwick, MA 01077
www.aminkpublishing.com

AM Ink Publishing and its logos are trademarked by AM Ink Publishing.

The publisher is not responsible for websites (or their content) not owned by the publisher.

Published in the United States of America.

Golden Linings

Tiny Tales about Pets, for Pets

Edited by
Carol M. Ford

Graphic Design by
Darin M. Peters

Our Mission

To help animals in need.
Author proceeds from sales of *Golden Linings* are donated
to animal rescue organizations and shelters.

Official Endorsement

We gratefully acknowledge the following for officially endorsing *Golden Linings*.

Introduction

When I started *Golden Linings*, I wasn't sure what to expect. As an animal lover and advocate, I always want to help animals in need, and over the years, I've made charitable donations to various animal shelters and rescue groups. I've also adopted cats and dogs. I wanted to do more, but realistically, I don't have the space to bring another pet into my home or to donate in large amounts.

What I *do* have, however, is a publisher who believes in my writing and goals, and a graphic artist I've worked with for over two decades. So I started brainstorming ideas. I reached out to my publisher, and to my family, friends, and colleagues who share my love for animals.

And *Golden Linings* was born.

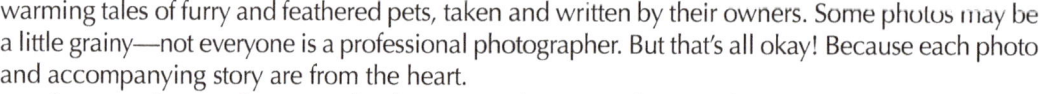

Within these pages are photographs and heart-warming tales of furry and feathered pets, taken and written by their owners. Some photos may be a little grainy—not everyone is a professional photographer. But that's all okay! Because each photo and accompanying story are from the heart.

Some stories are about pets that have passed on, over the "Rainbow Bridge," and those who submitted these contributions had a difficult time writing their piece. I give these individuals so much credit. The intense grief they felt while working on this book, even though years may have passed since their pet died, humbles me. It is a testament to how much they loved—and still love—their pets, and how deeply pets can impact our lives. Pets literally become members of the family.

Some were unable to contribute anything, simply because the pain of writing about their deceased pet was too much to bear. I understand and can relate. I've been there before and will be again, and I'm not sure I could have contributed to this book under the circumstances.

Pets love us unconditionally. They provide great joy and also great comfort. It's no wonder they are brought into schools, nursing homes, hospitals, and other public centers to offer a soft, gentle touch to children and adults who are struggling. I know when I'm going through a tough time, my two fur-kids—Copper and Charley—give me ongoing therapy, and by default, strength. They do this every single day, whether they realize it or not.

The goal of *Golden Linings* is to raise money for animals in need, and all author proceeds will be donated to animal rescue organizations and shelters. Your purchase of *Golden Linings* will help make a difference to end an animal's suffering or find a forever home.

On behalf of all who contributed and my publisher, I hope you enjoy this book, and I thank you so very much!

Carol M. Ford
Editor, *Golden Linings*

Special thanks to Michael Aloisi and AM Ink Publishing, and to graphic artist Darin Peters for helping me make this book a reality.

To all who contributed photographs and stories of your pets, thank you for participating. You have my deepest gratitude and respect.

To all of my friends, thank you for your friendship and support. Always know I'm glad you're in my life!

And finally, to my family—my parents Bob and Jan Ford, my sister and brother-in-law Barbara and Jeff Reim, and my nephews Ben Reim and Adam Reim—thank you for always being there for me. I love you all.

Chloe the Cat

Hi, I'm Chloe. The most important thing to know about me is that I *looooooove* being outside, even though I'm an indoor cat. I know all the small dogs on the block by smell and have rubbed my scent on many of the humans on the block, too. My mom takes me out, on a leash of course, and I greet whoever we pass with "meow, meow" and a headbutt to the knee.

In the beginning, my mom let me outside *without a leash!* She thought it was cool seeing me outside because for the first two years of my time with her, I was an indoor cat *only*. I enjoyed sitting at the screen door and talking to the birds and squirrels. Yes, I've mastered chirping.

But my mom learned fast to put me on a leash. One day, I climbed up in the tree out front where the birds and the squirrels live. I liked it up there *soooo* much, but my mom was crying the whole time. Eventually, a big red truck came down the street with sirens and a huge ladder! Then four men in yellow suits climbed up it and unhooked my leash from the branch. I still didn't want to go down, but there were a lot of people waiting on me! Finally, I climbed down to a huge crowd lining the street watching.

You might ask how I got up in the tree if I was on a leash? Well, mom used to let go of it when I walked behind the bushes so I didn't get stuck and tangled in them. This particular day, I laid down under the bushes, and when mom wasn't looking, I darted as fast as I could up that tree I had always dreamed of. I went up and up and up. Since then, my mom *never* lets go of the leash, *and* I'm not allowed to walk behind bushes.

She still lets me climb trees though!

**Translated from Meowish to English by:
Corrine Ochipinti**

Maizy

Maizy is our seven-year-old, very lovable furbaby. She is an Aussiedoodle – part Poodle and part Australian Shepard. Maizy has the ability to make everyone smile. She loves her treats, especially bananas and peanut butter pretzel nuggets. She will stare at the pantry door until one of her humans opens it for her to bump the container of nuggets with her nose!

When Maizy hears the car keys, she's ready at the door jumping up and down waiting for her ride. She loves her car rides! She knows when Tuesday nights roll around because that is when her Poppop visits. She waits at the door looking out the side window waiting for Poppop to come with his pockets filled with special treats. Maizy helps us with dinner clean up duties, too! When dinner is over, she bumps her Mama to tell her to load the dishwasher. She loves to help clean the dishes! Two of Maizy's favorite days are Christmas and her birthday. She can sniff out which wrapped gifts are hers. She carefully tears and discards the wrapping paper off with her teeth without hurting the gift inside!

Maizy has a few friends outside; her favorite furry friend is Lilly, who lives on the other side of our fence. They run back and forth along the fence every day. Of course, there are the squirrels and rabbits that she chases away! Once she even chased a skunk – we were not very happy with Maizy that time!

Maizy has a few dislikes as well. Mr. Hoover, our vacuum, is not her friend. She barks at him whenever we bring him out to clean. Maizy dislikes baths and having her nails cut, for sure, but she's very playful when it's all over and done. At the end of the night, she sleeps at the foot of the bed, usually with one of her human sisters. They hear the occasional grumble or groan from Maizy when she has to move to make room for them.

Maizy is happy to be part of our family, and we are happy she is ours!

Denise Centola

Ellie

In September 2003, I learned a litter of kittens was born in a lumberyard not far from where I lived, and the kittens were "Free to Good Home." I rode over to take a look, and there were two spunky little kittens left. One was just a bit more rambunctious than the other, and that was the "Stinky Little Girl" that came home with me in a cardboard box. I named her Ellie after a friend who had recently passed away from cancer.

Ellie was a love, but she was also a wild child! She had tiger stripe markings, and they suited her. She had a racing stripe down her back, but she also had a "worry brow." Ellie would tear all around the house at top speed, and she didn't sleep much. I had to work really hard with Ellie and be very patient with her because she could be a handful. But I understood her, and because of that, she trusted me completely.

But little did I know that Ellie had a ticking time bomb inside her. On a warm Sunday in October 2006, Ellie was sitting in the window watching nature and warming herself in the morning sun. I was working at the computer when I saw her fall out of the window and onto the floor, where she started flopping around like a fish. I believed she was having a seizure, so I quickly called the vet, and we raced at top speed to the vet hospital so she could get treatment.

I was prepared for Ellie to have to go on seizure medication, but I was unprepared for what would actually happen that day. Once we got there, Ellie did not improve. Instead, her condition worsened. They took her to one of the operating rooms, and soon, a technician came to tell me I had to make a decision—they wanted me to consent to put her down. They said I had to hurry because she was in so much pain. I gave the consent, but they couldn't prepare the needle fast enough. Ellie died from an aneurysm within forty-five minutes of falling out of the window. She was just three years old.

Ellie lived just a short little life, but it was a good little life. In those three short years, she was my buddy. My little partner in crime. My Stinky Little Girl who liked to race. When I think of Ellie, I am reminded that life is so short. We should live each day to its fullest and as if it is our last.

Carol M. Ford

The Magpies

There's a certain peace to be had that comes from being in sync with a creature of nature that has no ties to you or your home. In the case of the magpie family, it's that feeling they could be anywhere, but they choose to be with me.

Mama Magpie walked up to me while I was at the car one day, unloading groceries. She was curious and looking for a handout. Or not. Four years later, I have met and known Papa Magpie, and four sets of children, variously known as Peep, Little Peep, Bigfoot, Lumpy, Baby, and repeated variations thereof. I've helped when Mama's beak was broken and when she got carelessly discarded fishing wire wrapped around her neck, and when Papa broke his wing.

They've moved a few houses down the street now, a territorial argument that left me with a different magpie family living in my back yard. But I still go to see them most days. When Papa, who can't fly anymore, sees me, he comes running—literally. He meets me partway to our feeding point, and we walk the rest of the way together. Mama flies in and sits on my lap. Both eat out of my hand, and they've taught their babies that I'm nothing to be afraid of, and I have even fed them perched on my foot.

They are always the ones in control—they can touch me. I feel their feet, their beaks, and sometimes the back of their tails on my leg. But I can never touch them.

They look me right in the eye. They are wild, but they know they can trust me. There's a peace that comes with that. And a joy of quiet understanding.

Linda J. Groundwater

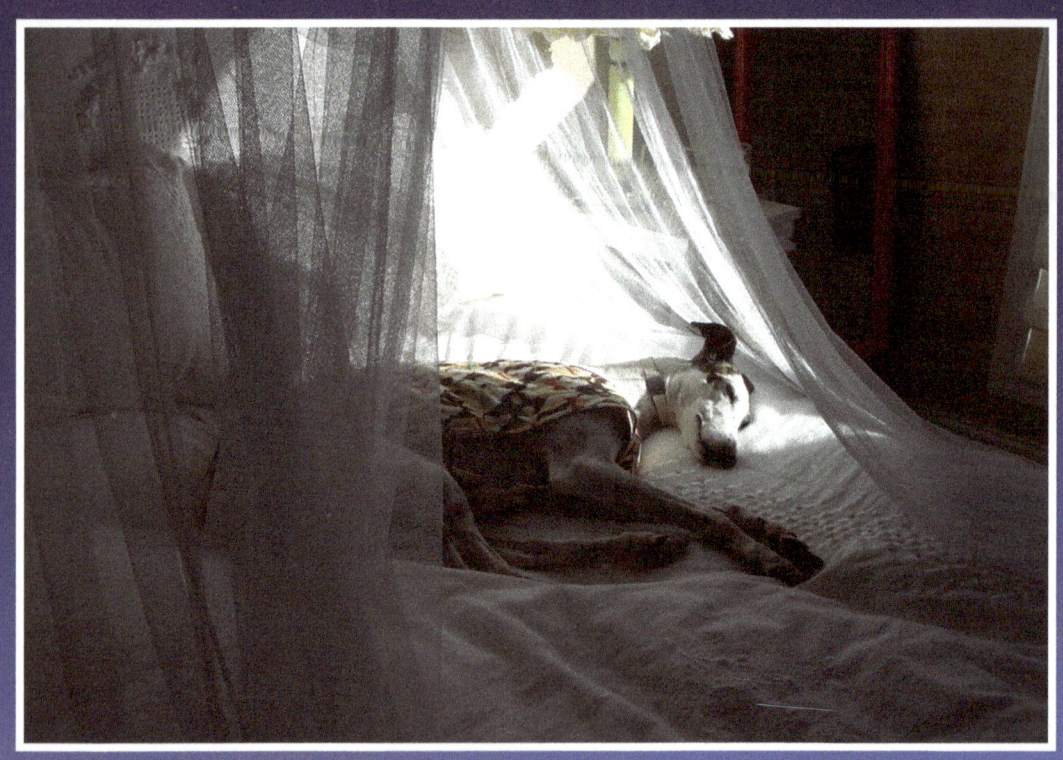

 Jenny

Jenny was a greyhound who came into my life when she washed out of her "schooling" as she was being trained to race. The only records I could find said she "showed no interest," which typically means they don't quite get the hang of chasing a stuffed rabbit around the track. Smart dog. She was eighteen months old when I adopted her and the most playful of all the greyhounds I've owned, possibly because she never did experience a career on the track. Jenny had baskets of stuffed toys throughout the house, and when company would come to visit, she would grab a toy in her mouth to go greet them.

Where she did love to chase bunnies was in her dreams. One of her favorite places to nap was on my mom's canopy bed, where she would bask in the sunbeam coming in through the window. She would fall deeply asleep, and her feet would begin to twitch as she raced in dreamland trying to catch those silly rabbits. She's since left for the Rainbow Bridge, and I like to think she and the bunnies have struck up a mutual friendship where they play together, chasing each other around and having a grand time until I get to see her again.

Kathleen Miritello

The Three Stooges

My fascination with the Three Stooges started at a very young age. I even got to meet Moe Howard himself in 1974, about a year before he died. Ever since then I have enjoyed their genre of slapstick comedy. They always make me laugh—as do my three cats.

With that being said, I had hoped to one day have three cats and name them after the Stooges. It wasn't until later in my adulthood I was able to adopt three cats that fit into the mix in hopes of them taking on their perspective personalities of their namesake. My cats' names are Moe, Larry, and Curly, and they have grown very accustomed to their names. Moe is the white cat with black markings. Curly is the tuxedo cat who is black with a white bib and white whiskers, and Larry is the all-black cat. How appropriate that all three cats are monochromatic (black and white) like the old shorts starring the Stooges.

Moe is the oldest cat, with Curly following second and Larry the youngest. They all get along so well with each other. From time to time, they play, and some slapstick is incurred. Bust most of all, they snuggle and give each other baths. I can say that I do give them nicknames such as knucklehead, porcupine, or chowderhead from time to time. I love my knuckleheads and enjoy bragging about them.

Darin M. Peters

Clancy

Clancy, our Irish Setter, was usually a very intelligent city dog who loved our RV trips around Australia. Once, when we were camping in the Australian Outback, Clancy spotted several birds in the distance.

"Ahhh! These look fun to chase!" he must have thought to himself!

So off he went, tearing through the long grass in pursuit. He ran like the wind until about half way, where his pace gradually slowed to a mere trot. As he got closer, and the birds appeared bigger, he slowed further, and as the real size of these enormous birds became apparent to him, he came to a complete stop. It didn't take him long to realize how much the six-foot-tall emus towered over him. As cool as he tried to appear, he couldn't hide a sheepish look as he turned on his heels and sprinted back to the safety of his family, leaving a cloud of dust behind him. All that exertion wore him out, and the next day, he just lounged around the camp, getting cuddles and resting his tired muscles.

Pauline Callaghan

Sable

I've had Sable for a little over four years now, and each day with him is a blessing. He is a ball of energy and constantly putting a smile on my face. When I come home from school or work, he is one of the highlights of my day. He's always at the door ready to greet me and receive lots of hugs and kisses.

He's my dog, and he's also one of my best friends. When I'm sad or stressed out, he's always there to cheer me up by sniffing the clothes I'm wearing and licking my face. Everyone who meets Sable agrees with me and says he's the sweetest dog ever. Visitors at my house always fall in love with him and his sweet-natured and silly personality.

One of my favorite things about Sable is that he will randomly lie down and rub his face across the carpet. He absolutely enjoys it, and I laugh every time he does it. Anything Sable does never gets old with me. He is one very special canine companion, and I could not ask for a better dog than Sable. He's my whole world, and I like him some days more than people!

I love you so much, Sable! I thank God everyday that you came into my life and can't wait to make many more memories with you for many more years!

Kaitlin Conroy

Walter

About four years ago, I started a job working from home, and while it's amazing to work in your pajamas, there's a lot people don't tell you. Like how there's no one there to shut the lights off and tell you work is done for the day, and gone are the days of celebrating holidays or lunch dates with coworkers. I really started to miss this aspect of being in an office, but found comfort and camaraderie in a different type of coworker—the furry kind.

Walter, my now five-year-old Cavalier King Charles Spaniel, spends his mornings with me in my home office. But once the day gets going, and phone calls and work start to take over, it apparently gets to be too much for him, and he needs a nap. Throughout the day, I can find him literally tucked into bed or sleeping in the sun in different rooms. One of the most common jokes my husband and I make to each other is, "What is he so tired from!?"

It's not like he's working a full-time job, or worrying about paying the mortgage and bills each month. He doesn't know the stresses of *adulting*; managing family, friends, commitments, work, life in general.

But that's almost what's so calming about having him in the house with me during the workday. He's there for a hug after a tough meeting; he's there for a walk when I need to get away from a computer screen. And it reminds me that his "job," which he does so well, is providing unconditional love every moment of every single day. And hey, that's got to be exhausting! But in today's world, it's something we all could use a little more of.

So go ahead and nap on, Walter. You deserve it.

Erin Salvatore Fisher

Rocky and Shorty

I was sitting at home one Saturday crying because we just had to have our dog Junior put down. There was a knock at the door; a little boy asked if I wanted this little dog. He said he found it in my driveway. He asked his grandmother if he could keep it, but she said no. I told him I would take him even though I said I wouldn't get another dog. I thanked the boy and brought the puppy in the house. A few seconds later, my son David from Michigan popped his head around the corner and said, "I got you, Mom!"

You see, the little boy was his girlfriend's son, with the made-up story of finding the puppy. My son had not known we had Junior put to rest, but he said something in the middle of the night told him I needed that puppy. We named him Rocky, and he was the sweetest, most lovable dog. He was always by my side and gave many kisses. And Rocky was a good boy when he had to have laser treatment for his eyes.

When Rocky was two years old, we decided to get another Yorkie. We drove to Delaware, and the breeder had two puppies left. We decided to take the male puppy, and we named him Shorty. On the ride home, Rocky licked him from head to toe, so by the time we got home, Shorty was soaking wet from all the kisses! I guess you could say they liked one another!

The two of them were inseparable. They slept next to one another and just played and played. They were such a joy to have. Yorkies are the best. They have great personalities, and their little tails never stop wagging!

Rocky lived to be eighteen-and-a-half years old, and Shorty lived to be thirteen-and-a-half years old. I miss them both very much, but I know they are in playing together in doggie Heaven and looking down on me.

Margaret Fox

Paco, Paco, Paco

How can words express love and companionship? Well, this is what I receive on a daily basis with my Mexican Red-Crowned Amazon Parrot, Paco.

We've been together now for more than nineteen years. His life expectancy could pass fifty years, so we plan on growing old together.

Paco is non-verbal due to his first year of life traveling from pet store to pet store. Language is often developed within the first year with verbal training and vocal stimulation. Since Paco was not "purchased" within that time frame, he didn't have any typical mimicking or learned English words. That didn't stop me from falling head over heels for him.

Paco communicates with me in endless ways—through whistles, sounds, grunts, moans, eye dilation, and body language. He's potty trained and has full flight.

Being a parrot parent, patience and commitment are key. Paco trusts me and looks forward to seeing me any time of the day. Our communication is comical at times. A typical morning consists of Paco becoming excited through song when he sees me open my bedroom door. He'll fly onto my shoulder and assist me in the kitchen as I make coffee. We'll look outside into the back yard to see if any of his feathered cousins are snacking on their bird feeder.

Although happy to be hanging out with me, Paco shows jealously when my attention is shown elsewhere. He'll verbally express himself by growling or with a high-pitched scream. Sometimes, my partner and I feel like we're living with a pterodactyl! For the most part, Paco is a Momma's Boy and is spoiled, and he contributes to ninety percent of any given conversation.

Having a pet, no matter the species or breed, is a life-long commitment. I would encourage fostering or adopting those that need homes. The love and companionship you'll receive will be priceless.

Cheryl Kiel

Copper

The day I brought Copper home on October 26, 2013, I didn't realize that this bundle of fluffy, golden fur whimpering in my lap in the backseat of the car would become my best friend. I have owned dogs before, but Copper is the first dog I raised and trained from puppyhood. We bonded quickly, and now, at almost five years of age, he is as loyal as can be to me.

Copper and I are the best of friends. Except for when I go to work or run errands or go places where the "no dogs allowed" rule is in place, we are joined at the hip. We go for long walks, and everyone on our route knows Copper! And he knows everyone! He is like the Mayor of the Neighborhood! We roughhouse. We play hide and seek. We go on excursions. When I come home from doing some shopping, I'll say, "I got you something!" And he charges into the kitchen, looking in all the bags until he finds his new toy. He has a million toys, and just watching him play can brighten my mood in a heartbeat. He even "talks," using a whole vocabulary of different barks, grunts, whines, and other vocal rumblings that hold a variety of meanings.

And when I'm faced with disappointments and haunted by painful memories, I hug Copper tightly, letting his fluffy coat catch my tears. During those times, he sits next to me, stoic, although a little worried, allowing my grief to pass.

His big, brown, soulful eyes express only love, innocence, happiness, and trust. There isn't a mean bone in his oversized body. A gentle giant, Copper allows even the smallest of children to pet him and sometimes tug on his ears or tail. He doesn't even flinch.

Copper is my hero. He is a soft reminder that even when life becomes overwhelming and a little bit scary, not to ever give up. Goodness exists in the world. Copper is living proof of it.

Carol M. Ford

Reece Rea

Reece was born in a barn in Kansas and put up for adoption at PetSmart. I found her there buried under her three brothers and the smallest of the bunch. She looked up at me and gave me a look that said, *Please help me! My brothers are crushing me!* She weighs only ten pounds now, but she eats constantly! She even gobbles up what her siblings leave behind.

I knew immediately that she was to come home with me. She is now fifteen years old, and she shares my home with her sister, Roxie, and her brother, Murphy. She is the Mama of the group! She always makes sure that her brother and sister are well groomed, warm, cuddled, and safe with her. When she is happy, her purr is so loud—it sounds like a small engine with a whistle!

She is the sweetest little kitty anyone could ever have had been blessed to know!

Adrienne Rea

Midnight

Ten years, two operations, fifty-three insurance claims, and still Midnight throws her toys, runs like a mad thing, and smiles. We got her when she was eight weeks old. She didn't know she'd been dumped when she was half that age, or that she'd struggle with her hips and knees. Or that she'd be what must be the happiest dog on earth. All she knew was that she had a home.

From the day she joined the family, she made us laugh. She jumped on the trampoline, made a toy of the broom head, and ran figure-eights around the yard. A few things have changed with age, but not many. She still expects me to play with her every night, throwing the ball or playing chase (I'm not always sure who's chasing whom), and when she gets particularly excited, she still throws her rawhide bone in the air and morphs into a canine slide by taking an enormous play bow. If she feels I have not played enough with her by the time I go to bed, she comes up beside me, sticks her nose in my face, and quite verbally tells me so. Her big brown eyes can't be ignored. So I drag myself out from between the sheets and give her a bit more attention.

Am I being bossed around by a furry kid? Maybe. Okay, yes. I'm sure I am. But she is a reminder of the power of joy. Of connection. Of living in the now. Apparently, I make her life happy, and she wants to spend as much time as possible with me. But what I give to her, she gives back to me tenfold. She needs very little to make her happy, and that's a lesson for me. Life is good. Period.

Linda J. Groundwater

Joey

Joey is our Russian Blue and almost the complete opposite of his foster brother, Buddy. Joey is our most vocal cat and routinely follows us around the house (as if he never gets any attention). He rarely stops moving for more than a few minutes; in fact, we're not entirely sure that he sleeps.

Joey is also a very sensitive cat whose greatest joy is sitting in your lap. Of course, getting him to settle down is another story; he'll walk around the different areas of your body for a while with his "peg legs" before finding a comfortable spot.

When he's not getting harassed by Buddy, Joey enjoys perching on the highest level of the cat tree so he can overlook the living room. We often call him our "bear" because he stands up on his hind legs like a grizzly when he wants your hand to meet the top of his head.

Joey has a funny meow that sounds half human and half like a wailing electric guitar. Like Buddy, he was also feral as a kitten but has since become the most domesticated house cat in history. When he decides to play, he will grab one of his toys and roll around with it before kicking it repeatedly with his back foot.

Read Buddy's story on page 47.

Gary Sweeney

Carlton

Our English Setter, Carlton, was a gentle soul, full of love and personality. Whenever we were out with him, people would stop us to remark on what a charming and gorgeous fellow he was. One of our most treasured memories of him was the day he brought a special magic to our wedding by being our ring bearer. At first, he was confused by all the activity, but always willing to please and dressed with bow tie and ring pouch, he was led down the aisle to the absolute delight of our guests. Normally shy, he relished being a part of the happy festivities. Luckily, I had a wrap to cover the mark when he jumped up to give me a kiss. We both felt so blessed to share this special day with him.

One dark night, we were walking with him along the river, and he was so surprised by a couple sitting on the grass that he jumped in the air and fell off the embankment into the river. It took us a moment to realize that the big splash was actually our ring bearer! A very embarrassed and wet Carlton had to be guided back up the steps!

Pauline Callaghan

Murphy Rea

This wonderful little guy joined my home after someone in my neighborhood put him out to fend for himself.

All Murphy wanted was a nice, warm home and a good meal. He was so happy to have been brought inside that he showed his gratitude immediately. He is the happiest cat you could ever want to meet. He prances around the house with such jubilation! He has snuggled up with his new sister, Reece, and he vocalizes his happiness with what almost sounds like words.

Murphy had a run in with a lawn mower several years ago, and he lost three toes on his front paw. It certainly doesn't slow him down though!

He has become one of the loves of my life, and he has never let me forget how lucky I am for bringing him into my life.

Adrienne Rea

Maggie

I was on the other side of the country, and a Facebook posting from a local rescue called for a temporary foster for a Golden Retriever en route to Pennsylvania. We had never fostered a dog, I wasn't coming home for two days, and my husband was juggling work and the kids' school and sports schedules. Without hesitation, I responded that we would foster.

The next morning, my husband picked up a sweet, well-mannered Golden Retriever named Sally. We were accustomed to houseguests, as we had hosted inner-city children from New York, an exchange student from Germany, and now it was time for Maggie, our Golden Retriever, to step up and become a canine host. Sally resided with us for four days, and Maggie led us through our first foster experience like a champion.

Over the years, Maggie has been a foster friend to dogs of all breeds and ages. The puppies tired her out, and she was patient with the post-partum moms. Maggie served as a leader when dogs that had been raised outside needed to learn inside manners or house training. As a foster, our family has been asked about the challenge of saying goodbye. You anticipate saying goodbye will be difficult until you meet the excited humans. Maggie always missed her canine companions more than we did.

Maggie is getting older, so we are taking a pause from fostering to attend to her health needs. Yet there is no doubt that Maggie's gentle mentorship is being paid forward by her canine foster friends living in our community. After Maggie crosses the Rainbow Bridge, we will continue Maggie's legacy by once again fostering. And maybe for the first time, we will be the excited humans who will choose not to say goodbye to our foster friend.

Tamara M. Kear

Joy

This is Joy. She is a retired racing greyhound who came into my life four months after having to put to sleep my previous greyhound due to osteosarcoma. Each time I've had to let go of a four-legged companion, it leaves a hole in my heart, but I also believe my heart expands a bit with the pain to make room for another dog.

Joy raced at Birmingham, Alabama, and she definitely lives up to her name. When she came into my life, she filled it with joy through her funny personality–her love for walkies, her silly helicopter spins, and her special fondness for shredding paper towels, preferably those stolen from the lap of one of her humans. I've owned four different greyhounds over the past twenty years, and they each have a slightly different personality but also share in common their "couch potato" nature. Some of us refer to them as "warm sculpture," for they will adorn your house by finding the softest rug, bed, or couch, and claiming it as their own.

Kathleen Miritello

Buddy

Buddy was being fostered by a woman in upstate Virginia when I adopted him and his "brother" Joey in 2012 (the two had bonded in foster). Buddy's life prior to that had been anything but comfortable. He was a feral cat living in a field and was routinely shot at for target practice. Luckily, he was never hit.

Since we added him to our family, Buddy has easily become our laziest boy! He enjoys curling up in the sunlight on the lowest level of his cat tree and sneaking up to the bedroom after dinner to take private naps. He hops down the steps like a rabbit and will often be caught staring at you for an extended period of time—earning him the rightful nickname, "The Watcher."

Buddy is a great cat to photograph because he doesn't run or move when the camera is on him, so we've been able to get many great shots of him doing absolutely nothing. One of our funniest memories is when Buddy saw Joey occupying the cat bed that he wanted—so he stood over him and glared patiently. When he decided that enough time had gone by, he playfully nipped at the back of Joey's neck to make him leave. After Joey took off, Buddy proceeded to wipe the bed clean with his paw before getting in and lying down.

Read Joey's story on page 37.

Gary Sweeney

Rama

Oh Rama, Oh Rama ou es-tu ?
Je te cherche partout!
J'entends le vents qui chuchote,
Dans cette belle nuit lunatique.
Je t'appelle du plus profound de mon coer,
Je t'attend a tous les coin du murs.
Je ne partirai pas demain, ni appres demain
Jusqu a ce que tu reviennes
Tu as traverse le monde loin de ton pays de naissance
Des Phillippines, jusqua Abu Dhabi
Enfin en France, ou tu te repose
Endorrmi profondement, endormi a poings ferme.

This poem was a product of my grief from losing my beloved cat in 1988, whom I missed so much. In this poem, I am expressing my longings for him. Rama was a seal point Siamese, born in the Philippines. The first time he came home to be adopted, we noticed his love of fish. He was a fun-loving cat who was also very curious and funny. I can't forget when he slipped at the edge of the pool and got wet, he didn't seem to mind. When we first moved to Abu Dhabi, I noticed he made funny noises while following the workers who came to the house. He was fascinated with the new language they were speaking. To him, it sounded different from Tagalog (Philippine language). When he wanted to go out from a closed door, he would jump onto the door handle and manage to go out.

He was very adventurous, a fighter to other cats outdoors. He would come home with wounds very often.

If I have to go back in time, I would not have allowed him to be an outdoor cat. Because of it he contracted a virus that led to his death in the end.

Juditha Zito

Note: Poem translates to: How I'm calling and looking for him in the bottom of my heart, under the full moon in the breeze of night (as I've always done). I would wait and wait in all corners of the wall. I would not leave then, even after tomorrow, until he would come back. He has travelled far from his country of birth, the Philippines, to Abu Dhabi. And finally, in France, where he now rests. Sleep tight and sleep profoundly.

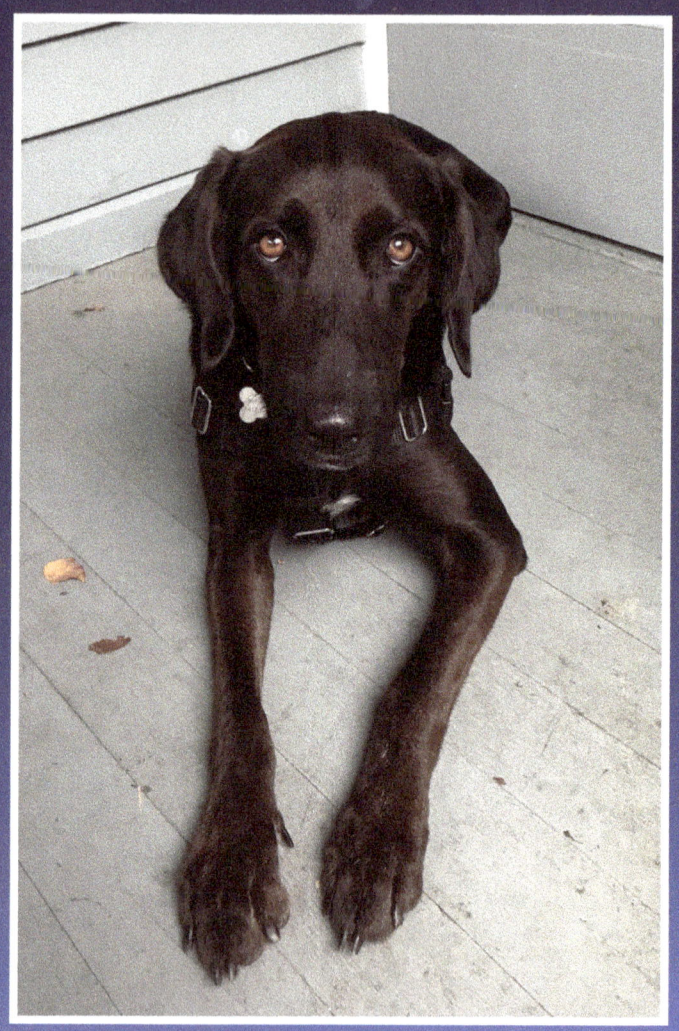

Daisy

The year 2017 was quite a time for us in so many ways. For our family, the year began with sadness, when our beloved Bob, a lab mix we rescued from a local shelter, died at the age of twelve years. The climate of sadness turned to chilling fear as we sat by our son's bedside in a hospital in San Francisco after his surgery for a ruptured cerebral aneurism. While there, my friend called to say she was losing her battle with breast cancer. She died in July. My brother's death followed in August. Threaded through these sad and scary personal times was the knowledge that our country was quickly deteriorating before our eyes, and that there seemed to be very little anyone could do about it. A deep melancholy seeped through me.

One October morning, after once again awakening to the now familiar dread of what the news would bring, I said to my husband, "I want a dog. I know we said we would wait awhile, but I want a dog by Christmas." He said, "I'm ready, too."

We began cruising the rescue sites and finally found our new little love—a year-old lab mix with soulful eyes who was found pregnant wandering through a field in North Carolina. Lucky Dog Rescue located homes for her puppies and treated her for heartworm. Now it was her turn to begin her new life.

We brought her home and named her Daisy, after my Irish grandmother. The house immediately felt different, a home with joy again after so much darkness. We take long walks together, and Daisy's curiosity reminds me to slow down, to take notice of and be grateful for the beauty around me. With Daisy curled up on the sofa with us in the evening and snuggled up in our bed at night, our home feels right again.

With time and some luck, perhaps the world will, too.

Judy Rollins

Roxie Rea

Roxie was born in a barn in Kansas. I found her at an adoption event in Olathe, Kansas, and I knew she needed to come home with me. She put her little paws outside of her cage and licked my hand. She was ten weeks old and full of spirit.

I named her Roxie because she showed such "moxie!" She is now fifteen years old and has brought such amazing *love!* Roxie climbs into bed with me and cuddles up to my head and neck, and she purrs the loudest purr you could imagine!

She is so tenacious! When she decides she wants something, she does not give up until she has accomplished it.

This photo is her claim to fame. My Roxie Girl won 2nd Place in *Yankee Magazine's* most beautiful cat contest!

Adrienne Rea

Edgar

We adopted "Hopper" as a kitten from the Richmond SPCA in September 2015 after losing one of our cats, Duddits, to cancer. Duddits was a black cat, and since black cats are consistently avoided/ignored in shelters, we wanted to make sure that another black cat found a good home.

When we had our first visit with him, he was like a little ball of energy, darting around the room and getting into anything he could find. We brought him home that day and renamed him Edgar, after one of our favorite authors, Edgar Allan Poe (who incidentally wrote "The Black Cat").

Edgar is obsessed with the kitchen sink, and seemingly, with water in general. When the dishwasher is running, he will jump up on the counter and stare into the drain like he's trying to figure out how it all works. He loves flying around the house at warp speed for no apparent reason until he's tired enough to plop down on the living room floor. There are times when Edgar acts like a monkey and other times when he acts like a bat, so we've combined the two personas into his "monkey bat" nickname.

Despite being almost three years old, Edgar still meows like a kitten on occasion; other times (such as when he wants to get into a closed room), he sounds like a train whistle.

Gary Sweeney

Charley

It was about a week after I lost my cat Ellie to an aneurysm (read Ellie's story on page 13) when my friends told me I should get another cat. I didn't think I was ready for another cat so soon after Ellie's sudden death, but they were insistent. They found a cat available for adoption at the local shelter, and they sent me the link. Right away, I fell in love with the picture. So I said, "Okay, I'll go and look at this cat, but this cat *only*."

My coworker and friend Darin Peters volunteered at the shelter at the time, and he met me there after work. He brought the cat, whose shelter name was Flower, out of her crate and handed her to me. That was it! She wrapped herself all around me and purred nonstop. After about a half hour, I knew I had to have her. Within a couple of days, I brought her home.

I decided to rename her Charley. I had been working on Bob Crane's biography at the time. When Bob was on the air (he was a radio personality during the 1950s-1960s before *Hogan's Heroes*), he would often say to his listeners, "Well, hello there, Charlie!" or "Look out there, Charlie!" Ironically—and I didn't know this until much later—Bob Crane's best friend from school was Charlie Zito. Most likely, Bob was giving an on-air nod to him! I now say that I named Charley after Charlie, who became one of my dearest friends, in a roundabout, retrospective kind of way.

Charley is the sweetest cat and a real cuddle bug. Her fur is an iridescent grey, and her tail is fluffy, making her look like a silver fox. She sleeps with me every night, curling up under the covers, around my neck and chin, where she purrs herself to sleep. In the twelve years I've owned her, I've only ever heard her hiss once—when the neighbor's dog came up to the window to play, and he startled her.

Charley was diagnosed with feline immunosuppressive virus (FIV) on her first visit to the vet soon after I adopted her, so I can't have another cat right now. But that's okay. Copper, Charley, and I make a happy—albeit unique—little herd!

Carol M. Ford

Big Man

I had been finding hair ties strewn about the house not long after we adopted our beloved, 20-pound jokester of a cat, Big Man. In a house full of girls with long hair, hair ties come at a premium—having an out-of-control mane and nothing with which to tame it is high on my list of annoyances. I would get after my daughters for taking off with my hair ties, thinking they were using them as toys or with their dolls.

Until one day, home alone with Big Man, I heard a drawer in the bathroom slide open and the distinct sound of someone—some*thing*—rifling through the drawer full of hair goodies. I crept closer to the doorway and peered in, only to see Big Man perched on the toilet, hovering over the drawer and picking through its contents with his paws. He located a bright green hair tie, took it in his teeth, and off he went, excitedly trotting past me.

To this day, there is no safe place for hair ties in our house. They are Big Man's favorite toy, and he seeks them out relentlessly. Visitors now know that the mess of hair ties around the house isn't due to thoughtless children or poor housekeeping, but a happy kitty who just loves hair ties!

Sarah Black

Rama 2

Rama II was named after my first Rama (read Rama's story on page 49). We adopted him in the spring of 1994. I was given two choices of the litter. One was looking so healthy. Rama was looking so scrawny. I picked Rama because my heart felt that he needed more love.

During the first few days and weeks with us, he would get into our coats or shirts for warmth. Later on, it became one of his favorite pastimes. He was so skinny and couldn't contain the heat from his body. One day, I took him shopping at T.J. Maxx. Nobody knew he was inside my coat until he woke up and made a crying noise, and then they'd give me a puzzled look!

Rama II loved to be cuddled. He was crazy for corn and beans. We would take him out on a leash, and he loved catching crickets. Although he was born a runt of the litter, he grew up to be a spunk. He was a people cat because he was used to meeting different people every day.

My husband and I owned a taxi business from 1992 until 1996. We practically lived in the office 24/7. Rama came to the office with us every day. People who knew him loved to visit him while waiting for their train. Rama loved their attention, too. There was one particular person he was crazy about. We didn't know why he was so in love with our mailman, William. William admitted he was not particularly a cat person, but Rama couldn't wait to see him every day. He could sense William even from far away. All of a sudden, he would perk up from a deep sleep, and when his favorite mailman would show his face, he would start the "I'm so happy to see you" love. Poor Will could never leave right away!

Sadly, Rama only lived for two years due to a congenital heart failure. When he was at the vet hospital, I brought beans to perk him up, and I also called William, the mailman. That was a sad day for us because it was too soon to say goodbye to a spunky little guy.

Juditha Zito

Josie

My cat does not know how to cat.

I was told a cat would wake me up to eat. She wakes me up to snuggle. She's not looking for breakfast or playtime. She's not interested in my early meetings. Each morning, at the sound of my alarm, she'll roll over from the spot where she's nestled beside me and climbs on my chest so she can bury her head in my neck like a baby.

I was told a cat would sleep all day. She greets me when I come home by rolling over for a belly rub. She'll make one of two sounds: a contented purr that she's happy to see me. Or a drawn out mewl to let me know her favorite toy has been stuck under the couch since I left. I'll retrieve her prize, and then back to belly rubs like a puppy.

I was told a cat would mostly ignore me. She gives the best hugs. I learned this the morning after I adopted her. We sat on the floor together, trying to learn what to make of our new arrangement. Suddenly, she placed her paws on my knee, and made her way up until her head was resting on my shoulder, stretching her tiny body against mine, like a life-long friend.

I was brilliantly misled. She is a baby to fill my arms, a confidant to share my secrets, a roommate to liven my quiet apartment. She is funny and goofy, dramatic and fierce. I see the best and the worst of myself in her.

I have a cat that does not know how to cat. Her name is Josie, and she is so much more.

Rosaria Mineo

Inara

From the time I was born, my father always had a big, furry companion at home to love. Photos of my siblings and me as children almost exclusively depicted us napping with a dog, camping with a dog, sledding with a dog, swimming with a dog…and the list goes on. They were like brothers and sisters to me. Inara the pug, however, was *my* first dog—my first baby.

I was in my early 20s and still living at home when I told my dad I wanted to raise a pug. He laughed. He was accustomed to big, oafy, mixed breeds. At the time, we had a dalmation/mastiff named Cody who was about seven years old. "Cody will eat a pug. You know that, right?" my dad warned. Cody wasn't mean. He was just protective. And very large. But I knew Cody would accept another dog if it were mine. I just knew it. My father smirked, but he agreed. He could never say no to giving a puppy a good home, and that's when I learned what he always knew—a dog's love changes everything.

Inara (named after a character from *Firefly*, one of my favorite TV shows) was ten weeks old when I brought her home. Cody graciously mothered her, exactly as I knew he would. I made her a warm, fluffy bed inside an empty vacuum cleaner box. Her adorable little cries got the best of me though, and she's slept (snoring loudly) in my bed ever since.

When I look at my beautiful baby girl, now twelve years young with a grey face, I get a flash of bittersweet memories. She has known all of the best souls I've ever loved, and I wonder if she understands why some of them are now gone. My late grandmother, affectionately known as Punkin, had cried tears of joy when I brought Inara to see her for the first time. This was *my* baby and her great-grandpug. They bonded instantly. Inara was the light of my step-father's eye before he passed, and he had never been a fan of dogs before he met her. We lost Cody four years ago.

Every once in a while, if their names come up in conversation, Inara's ears still perk up. She looks at the door, hope in her eyes. Cody. Punkin. Harry. She's never forgotten them, and for me, part of them still lives on through her love.

Katie R. Rayburn

This little guy is in love with me! And I am in love with him!

RJ is a Coton de Tuléar, a breed of dog originating from the island country Madagascar, named for its cotton-like coat and the Madagascar city, Tuléar. On the day I brought him home as a puppy, he fell asleep right on my shoulder. RJ and I bonded right from the start, and we are inseparable. He follows me wherever I go.

He is exceptionally smart. He understands when I talk to him, nodding and tilting his head back and forth, taking in every word. He has different facial expressions and so many different sounds. It is like he is talking, with all the unique sounds he makes. When I wink at him, he even winks back!

We play all the time, and soccer is RJ's favorite game. Sometimes, we play with two soccer balls—these aren't real soccer balls, but soft dog toys. He will dash after the soccer balls as I kick them away, and despite his small size, he will carry all of them back to me at once!

We go for long walks every day. RJ is so tiny that he can't keep up, so he rides along on the walk in the stroller. He loves his stroller! When I say, "We're going for a walk," he immediately runs and jumps in the stroller. When it's cold out, he waits for me to put his little sweater on first.

RJ is a precious boy. He is my buddy. He is my best friend. I love him to pieces. He goes wherever I go. He is my happiness and brings me so much joy. I'm so happy this little boy is in my life.

Jan Ford

Harry

Harry. AKA Harold James. Puppy. The World's Oldest Dog. The World's Most Expensive Dog.

Harry was a rescue from the streets of Camden, New Jersey. He was skin and bones, but a happy puppy. He's nine years old now (and eighty pounds) and is a "good boy" who we love very much even though he sometimes doesn't smell very good.

Harry's patiently allowed nine nieces and four nephews poke and climb him. He greets every visitor with a few barks, some sniffing, and a wagging tail. He's part of our family and is always willing to be a snuggly nap buddy.

Jack Bryant and Kevin Shumaker

Rhymin' Simon

Rhymin' Simon is a two-year-old cat that has been in my home less than a month. Initially, he was scared because he had been a stray who was taken to a shelter for a brief time. Right now, Rhymin' Simon and I are getting to know each other better, and are learning each other's habits and likes. He is a playful cat who loves to be petted. Rhymin' Simon's favorite playtime activity is jumping up and down to grab cat toys on sticks.

I never realized cats have different personalities. My last cat, a female named Biscuit, was mainly a lounge cat, and she was eight years old when I got her. Biscuit, whose colors were also orange and white, lived until just a few days before the age of seventeen years. She passed on earlier this year.

Rhymin' Simon is a happy, playful, and friendly cat!

Bill Dillane

My lifelong love of rabbits began with Rosie, the first bunny to hop into my heart. I was a teen attending the state fair in the 1980s, admiring all the bunnies, when I saw her. She was a two-month-old, black-and-white Dutch rabbit looking for a home. I convinced my mother to let her leave with us on that hot August day, which wasn't difficult since my family loves animals.

Rosie adapted well to her new life, and I was excited to have a bunny. While she was a family member first and foremost, I thought I would try our luck in rabbit shows just for fun. Suffice it to say that Rosie wasn't destined for success in that area, and so her career ended before it even began. While she fell short in this regard, she excelled as the companion that I wanted. She enjoyed being held as I planted gentle kisses on top of her head, and sometimes, she would fall asleep as I stroked her soft, velvet ears. Rosie also enjoyed supervised romps in the backyard on nice days, and she never met a carrot she didn't like.

Rosie was loved and spoiled for the rest of her days. Although she has been gone for decades, and several rabbits followed in her memory, I still miss her. While a few new family members over the years included show bunnies, they were outnumbered by my other rabbits that were rescued or adopted from the shelter. My little Dutch bunny was perfect in her own way, and that's how I'll remember Rosie.

Loretta Sisco

Lola and Papi

In the summer of 1996, my now-ex-husband and I decided we wanted a dog. I started looking through the classified ads in the local paper, and within about a week, an ad appeared for two Shetland Sheepdogs (or Shelties), ages six and seven years, one male and one female. Lola and Papi were "free to good home," but because they were a bonded pair, they had to be adopted together.

I had loved collies ever since I was a little girl, and I jumped at the idea of adopting these two "miniature collies." My ex-husband and I drove over to the owner's home, but when we got there, we were shocked at what we saw. These two little dogs had been kept tied in the garage. With the exception of his face, Papi was completely shaven, and Lola was a trembling mess. They were in bad shape, and at the very least, were stressed and unhappy. I remember saying to my ex-husband, "We've got to get them out of here."

So we did. The owner unhooked them from the wall and handed us their leashes. A few kids rode by on bikes, and one said with a shrug, "Oh, the dogs are leaving?" I was amazed at their indifference and lack of care and concern.

Lola (in the front of the picture) and Papi adjusted quickly and were happy in their new home. They were the sweetest little dogs. Papi grew his full coat back, and their full personalities were allowed to develop. Papi was handsome and playful, while Lola was a princess. And Lola would give you these sideways glances and could really stare you down!

My ex-husband and I divorced a year later. Personally, it was a traumatic experience, but Lola and Papi were right there for me. They were the best little therapy dogs a person could have ever asked for, and they got me through that difficult time. Lola and Papi lived full, happy lives. Lola passed away in 2005 following a sudden seizure, and Papi died a year later, in 2006. But they're always in my heart. My ex-husband and I may have rescued them, but they, in turn, rescued me.

Carol M. Ford

Henry Ernest, Reggie, and Herbert

All was right in my world as long as Henry Ernest (pictured at top right) was by my side. He gave me a reason to get out of bed and go on living because he needed to be fed and to chase the squirrels. He'd gladly lick the tears from my face. And then I rescued his bigger brother Reggie (bottom right), who desperately needed love and someone to play with.

Seven years later, Reggie began having kidney failure all while I was struggling to keep Henry Ernest comfortable with a slowly collapsing trachea. They died just two months apart, with Christmas in the middle.

This was so difficult to write because the heartbreak is too much to realize.

However, the happier ending is that I rescued Herbert (pictured at far left) just one month later from a homeless woman, and now the cycle of unconditional love begins again.

Henry Ernest and Reggie are in my heart, always. And Herbert is in my heart, is my joy, and always right by my side!

Karen Crane

Mitz and Fritz

Mitz and Fritz were my fur "kids" and my fur "babies." In 2005, shortly after my cat Nutsy passed away, my husband, Doug, surprised me with two kittens—Mitz, all black with white markings, and Fritz, all white with black markings. I had just gotten home from work, and Doug was sitting there in the living room waiting for me with this little ball of fluff in his lap!

Mitz and Fritz were not littermates. They were cage mates, rescued by the small shelter our veterinarian maintained for stray or surrendered animals. Fritz was our Independence Day cat—born on the Fourth of July in 2005. Mitz was born a few months later, in September 2005. They had bonded in their cage, so we adopted them both together. Mitz came home a week before Fritz. Fritz had stomach problems, and the vet didn't want to release him right away until they knew he would be okay.

While Fritz had lifelong tummy troubles, Mitz had lifelong allergies. Ever since she was a baby, she was a sneezer. Mitz sneezed *all* the time—and all over the place! I would follow her around the condo cleaning up her kitty snots! My "kids" were playful and loved to antagonize each other—and us! But their claim to fame was that they were "Hall Cats." During the day, we'd leave the door to our condo cracked open so Mitz and Fritz could roam the hallway and visit with our neighbors. All of our neighbors loved them, and Mitz and Fritz would come and go and visit with each of them as they pleased. Whenever I'd come home from work, Fritz would greet me right at the elevator. He always knew when I was due to come home. The elevator doors would open on our floor, and there he would be!

I lost Doug, Mitz, and Fritz all within a few years of each other. I loved them so much and miss them all terribly. This was tough for me to do—to go through pictures and remember, but I'm glad I did.

Dee Young

Sophie and Sabrina

It had been several years since my husband, Bob, and I had owned a pet. When our kids were little and going through their teen years, we had all kinds of pets—a bird, fish, cats, and dogs. In fact, when I was young, my family always had pets, including horses. So in the summer of 2011, Bob and I decided to get a kitten.

We found an adorable litter of Persian kittens, and we fell in love with the tortoise grey runt, the smallest one of the litter. We chose her and named her Sophie. However, we soon learned the last available kitten in the litter had been refused. The person who was going to take her changed her mind and didn't want this kitten. So we decided to give this forlorn little kitten a home, too. We named her Sabrina.

Sophie and Sabrina are sisters in every sense of the word. They play together; sleep together; eat together. They become worried about each other. When one gets stuck in a closet, the other one will sit by the door and cry nonstop to let us know. They even both go see Santa and sit on his lap at Christmas! And just like human sisters, they also irritate each other. All Sabrina has to do is walk by Sophie, and Sophie will hiss for no apparent reason! It's the equivalent to the classic, "Mom, she touched me!" But they also love each other, and we love them.

Sabrina, sometimes called Bumble because she looks like a bumblebee due to all of her fur, is also in love—but not with another cat. She is in love with our dog, RJ! She follows RJ all around the house and will play with him. We believe Sabrina thinks she is a dog. (See page 67 for RJ's story.)

Our home has always been full of furry cuddle bugs, and Sophie and Sabrina have certainly brought a lot of cuddles, happiness, and love to our home!

Jan Ford

Millie

In 2012, we were searching through adoption sites online when we came across a photo of a scruffy little rescue pup the foster family had named "Baby Millie," so we went for a visit. Just a couple of months old, this Border Collie/Black Lab mix had a head that seemed too big for her body, with fluffy, unkempt tufts of hair around her ears and a spindly little tail. She was adorable. And one look into those big, brown, soulful eyes was all it took to know she was meant to be part of our family.

When we first brought her home, Millie liked to curl up and sleep in a little cardboard box we had for her toys. But that didn't last long. Millie grew. Her body caught up to her head, and her little tail filled out to become her big, fluffy pride-and-joy.

Millie was a very energetic puppy. It was a bit of a challenge to calm her down, when her instincts had her running in circles around us in the back yard, trying to get control of the "herd." But with a few months of patient training, Millie went from wild-child to a loyal and well-behaved "good girl." She was even certified as an official "Canine Good Citizen," passing her qualification test with flying colors.

Gentle and obedient, Millie is always friendly to strangers and never barks. Except at the mailman. Hey, nobody's perfect; besides, so far, every time she's barked, he's gone away, so clearly, she's doing her job!

She still loves to run, and is she ever fast! We call her "Black Lightning" as she zooms around the perimeter of the back yard at breakneck speed. Millie likes summer days, taking walks, ice cream, and playing with her canine cousins. And she loves her people. And we love her.

The Reim Family

Lulu

My given name is Lulu Belle, but my mommies call me Lu. People are always asking what breed I am, but that's because I'm unusual: I am half-Catahoula Leopard Dog, half-Pit Bull mix. Catahoulas are the state dog of Louisiana, and they are known for being hard-working but obstinate at times. It's true; when I get a hold of one of my toys, I love it to pieces...that is, until every ounce of stuffing is on the floor! When I take my Mama Jen for a walk, she'd better have her comfortable shoes on because I always want to be the leader. Of course, I don't always have to be active: I love to watch movies, catch an occasional episode of *Family Guy*, or zone out to dog T.V. But nothing—*nothing*—compares to taking a nice, long nap alongside Mama. (Mama Mindy and Auntie Becky say I snore, but I don't believe them.)

I'm a Scorpio, like Mama Jen, born in November of 2013. My mommies adopted me when I was just a pup from the Sadie Mae Foundation, a dog rescue in Connecticut. I came with a few health issues: in addition to battling a few bothersome skin allergies, I have to take Prion daily to keep my bladder in check and to have my kidney function monitored, and this pesky hip dysplasia bothers me every now and then. However, I don't let those things get me down. I try to savor the good things in life: biscuits and treats, hanging around with my cat sister Scarlette, and regular visits from my boyfriend Brody, a handsome Boxer who lives just down the street.

If you need fashion advice, you've come to the right place! I wear a different collar every month and coordinate my patterns with the holiday seasons. If you're looking for a little comfort, check the recliner. I like to sit like a human, so climb in next to me and snuggle...as long as you don't mind a few extra wet kisses!

**Translated from BowWowish to English by:
Jennifer Danio**

Carol M. Ford has more than twenty years of experience in the publishing industry. She earned her BA degree with Honors in English/Liberal Arts from Glassboro State College (now Rowan University) in Glassboro, New Jersey. She is the Director of Editorial Services, an editor, and a managing editor for Anthony J. Jannetti, Inc. (AJJ), a health care association management, marketing, and publishing firm located in southern New Jersey near Philadelphia. Working with leaders in the nursing community, she oversees the production of several clinical peer-reviewed nursing journals, publications, and textbooks. She is the author of *Bob Crane: The Definitive Biography*, which details the life of the late radio personality and *Hogan's Heroes* star, and is currently working on her next book. Visit Carol's website at www.carolmford.com.

www.ingramcontent.com/pod-product-compliance
Lightning Source LLC
Chambersburg PA
CBHW041140170426
43200CB00021B/2987